Animals

Dogs

by Nick Rebman

FOCUS READERS

FOCUS READERS

www.focusreaders.com

Focus Readers is distributed by North Star Editions:
sales@northstareditions.com | 888-417-0195

Produced for Focus Readers by Red Line Editorial.

Photographs ©: Ammit Jack/Shutterstock Images, cover, 1; Artem Kursin/Shutterstock Images, 4; Volodymyr Burdiak/Shutterstock Images, 7, 16 (bottom left); CyberKat/Shutterstock Images, 9, 16 (bottom right); Hurst Photo/Shutterstock Images, 11; Twinsterphoto/Shutterstock Images, 13; Alfa Photostudio/Shutterstock Images, 15; Robert Crum/Shutterstock Images, 16 (top left); beyhanyazar/iStockphoto, 16 (top right)

ISBN
978-1-63517-847-0 (hardcover)
978-1-63517-948-4 (paperback)
978-1-64185-151-0 (ebook pdf)
978-1-64185-050-6 (hosted ebook)

Library of Congress Control Number: 2018931095

Printed in the United States of America
Mankato, MN
May, 2018

About the Author

Nick Rebman enjoys reading, drawing, and traveling to places where he doesn't speak the language. He lives in Minnesota.

Table of Contents

Dogs

Dogs come in many sizes.

Some are very big.

Some are very small.

Dogs are covered with **hair**.

Dogs have four legs.

Some dogs have long tails.

tail
leg

Behavior

Dogs like to run.

They also like to **sniff**.

Their noses can smell many things.

nose

Most dogs live with people.
They live in houses
or **apartments**.
Their owners take care
of them.

owners

Food

Dogs eat dog food.
People buy dog food at
pet stores.
Dogs also need fresh water
every day.

dog food

Many dogs are friendly.

They make great pets.

Glossary

apartments

pet stores

hair

sniff

Index